My Shoes

Written by Lisa James

T0386050

Contents

Shoes

These are my shoes.
They are trainers.

There are lots of kinds of shoes.

Running Shoes

Some shoes are made for running. Running shoes have soft **soles**.

sole

4

Fast fact
Some running shoes have spikes to grip the ground.

Wellies

Wellies are made from rubber.
They keep your feet dry.

Fast fact

Waders are water boots. They go all the way up to your chest.

Tap Shoes

Tap shoes have metal on the bottom.
The metal taps when you dance.

metal plate

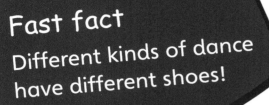

Sandals

Sandals keep our feet cool when it is hot. They keep the soles of our feet safe.

Fast fact

Sandals are perfect
for the beach!

Snow and Ice Shoes

Ice skates have a sharp **blade** on the bottom. The blade slides over the ice.

sharp blade

Fast fact

Snow shoes have a wide, flat bottom, so you do not sink in the snow.

Riding Boots

Riding boots are hard.
The toes go in the **stirrups**.

stirrup

Fast fact
Horses wear shoes made from metal.

15

Glossary

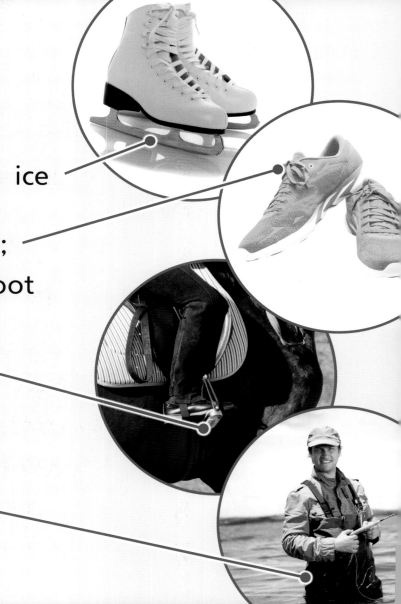

blade   part of a skate that slides on the ice

sole   bottom of a shoe; bottom of your foot

stirrup   loop that holds a rider's foot

waders   long boots for deep water